Out at night

Some living things just come out at night.
Can you think of some?

Bats

A bat's hearing can help it travel and get food in the dark.

Bats hang off things.
The wings have thin
fingers on them.

Wombats

Wombats have short legs and tails. They have teeth a bit like a rat's.

Fun fact: Wombats have odd looking poo!

They spend the night looking for food and digging. They feed on bark and roots.

Owls

An owl can see well in the dark. It can hear well too. It feeds on insects, frogs and lizards.

talons

Owls have big, strong, sharp talons. Talons help them to grab and kill the food they hunt.

Foxes

Foxes hunt at night. They have big ears to help them to hear.

Foxes feed on lots of things such as rats, insects, rabbits, frogs, seeds, eggs and lizards.

Look at the fox's tail. It is like a brush.

Moths

This is a bee-mimicking moth.

Is it a moth or a stick?

Moths are insects that you see at night. Some moths are good at mimicking things.

Here is an owl moth.

It is hard to see this moth.

Mimicking can help to keep them from harm.

Possums

This is a common brushtail possum.

Possums can be seen in woodlands, farmlands and in towns. You might hear them run on the roof! They can grunt and hiss too.

Here is a common ringtail possum.

Possums rest in the light and feed at night. They might munch on shoots, seeds and bugs in the garden.

The sun is going down
and some living things
are just getting up!

Words to blend

looking	good	poo
food	roots	night
hearing	hear	ears
short	tails	teeth
feed	bee	see
owls	down	sharp
dark	harm	hard

Before reading

Synopsis: While we are sleeping, there are many creatures that come out at night to hunt for food.

Review graphemes/phonemes: oo oo igh ear or ai ee ow ar

Story discussion: Look at the cover and read the title together. Ask: *What kinds of animals go out at night? How do you think they find their way around when it is dark?* Share children's predictions about some of the animals that might feature in the book. Check back on the predictions after reading, to see if they were correct.

Link to prior learning: Display a word with adjacent consonants from the story, e.g. *brush*. Ask children to put a dot under each single-letter grapheme (*b, r, u*) and a line under the digraph (*sh*). Model, if necessary, how to sound out and blend the adjacent consonants together to read the word. Repeat with another word from the story, e.g. *stand*, and encourage children to sound out and blend the word independently.

Vocabulary check: mimicking – copying the way something looks and/or acts

Decoding practice: Display the word *mimicking*. Show children how to split it into three syllables: *mim/ick/ing*. Together, sound out and blend each syllable in turn, to read the word.

Tricky word practice: Display the word *going*. Read the word, and ask children to show you the tricky bit (*o*, which makes the sound /oa/). Practise reading and spelling this word.

After reading

Apply learning: Ask: *Which animal in this book did you think was most interesting, and why?* Encourage children to find or recall an interesting fact about their chosen animal.

Comprehension

- Describe what a bat's wing looks like.

- What is unusual about wombat poo?

- What do owls eat?

Fluency

- Pick a page that most of the group read quite easily. Ask them to reread it with pace and expression. Model how to do this if necessary.

- Encourage children to choose a favourite page from the book and read it with appropriate pace and intonation.

- Practise reading the words on page 17.

Tricky words review

out	they	the
you	of	to
have	are	going
some	come	like
here	your	go